SHALL I COMPARE THEE?

10 Shakespeare settings for mixed voices

Compiled and edited by Bob Chilcott

MUSIC DEPARTMENT

UNIVERSITY PRESS

OXFORD
UNIVERSITY PRESS

Great Clarendon Street, Oxford OX2 6DP,
United Kingdom

Oxford University Press is a department of the University of Oxford.
It furthers the University's objective of excellence in research, scholarship,
and education by publishing worldwide. Oxford is a registered trade mark of
Oxford University Press in the UK and in certain other countries

Database right Oxford University Press (maker)

First published 2015

Impression: 1

ISBN 978-0-19-340614-8

Music and text origination by
Katie Johnston
Printed in Great Britain on acid-free paper by
Halstan & Co. Ltd, Amersham, Bucks.

Preface

In order to mark the four hundredth anniversary of the death of William Shakespeare, we have collected together ten newly composed settings of some of his most familiar words. Many singers all over the world will be familiar with so many of the songs in Shakespeare's plays through the work of composers such as Ralph Vaughan Williams, Gerald Finzi, Sir Michael Tippett, Frank Martin, and John Rutter, to name but a few. For this collection we have asked composers from Britain, Canada, and Finland to put their own stamp on Shakespeare's songs and texts—words that abound with energy and have so much singing line and rhythm within them; words that, in fact, are in most cases surely meant to be sung.

Our source for the texts, and for general reference, has been The Oxford Shakespeare edition, and we have been extremely lucky to have had guidance from Carol Rutter, Professor of Shakespeare and Performance Studies at Warwick University. I am also grateful to the estate of William Walton for allowing me to make a version for voices of his piece 'Touch her soft lips and part', taken from the 1947 *Two Pieces for Strings from 'Henry V'*. I would also like to thank Philip Croydon, Commissioning Editor at Oxford University Press, for his support and guidance on this book, and also Robyn Elton for her careful editing work.

In putting this collection together, I hope we have achieved our aim of creating a practical performance edition that can be used by choirs everywhere to celebrate the life and work of one of our greatest writers—as well as the music of some wonderful contemporary composers.

Bob Chilcott
June 2015

Also available from Oxford University Press:
Hark, hark, the lark: 8 Shakespeare settings for upper voices (978–0–19–340615–5)

Contents

Come away, come away death

William Shakespeare
from *Twelfth Night* (Act 2, Scene 4)

HOWARD SKEMPTON
(b. 1947)

Duration: 1.5 mins

one so true Did share it. Not a flo-wer, not a flo-wer

sweet On my black cof-fin let there be strown. Not a friend,

not a friend greet My poor corpse, where my bones_ shall be

thrown. A thou-sand thou-sand sighs to save, Lay me O where

Sad true_ lov - er ne-ver find my grave, To weep there.

for Chamber Choir Cantinovum and Rita Varonen

Fear no more the heat o' th' sun

William Shakespeare
from *Cymbeline* (Act 4, Scene 2)

JUSSI CHYDENIUS
(b. 1972)

Duration: 4.5 mins

Animated but steady

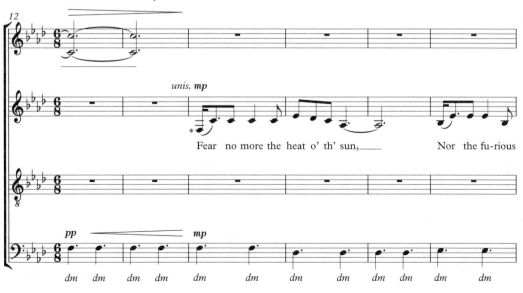

* The alto melody may be doubled by a few tenors, if desired.

Commissioned by the Agincourt Singers (James Pinhorn, Conductor)
in celebration of the one hundredth anniversary of the Agincourt Collegiate Institute

I know a bank where the wild thyme blows

William Shakespeare
from *A Midsummer Night's Dream* (Act 2, Scene 1)

SARAH QUARTEL
(b. 1982)

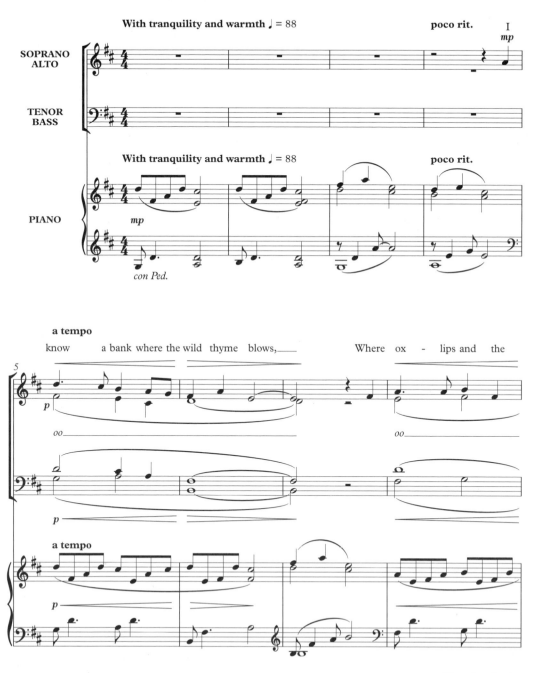

Duration: 3 mins

* *eglantine* = sweet briar, a species of wild rose

* *throws* = sheds
† *weed* = garments

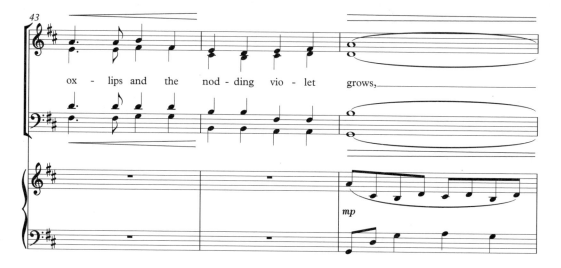

ox - lips and the nod - ding vio - let grows,_____

mp

_____ Quite o - ver - can - o - pied_____ with lus - cious

wood - bine,_____ With sweet musk -

mp

- ros - es,   and   with   eg - lan - tine._____   I

know   a bank where the wild   thyme   blows_____   the

wild   thyme   blows._____

poco rit.   *mf*   *mp*

poco rit.   *mf*

mp

rit.   *dim.*   *p*

dim.   *p*

rit.

mp   *dim.*   *p*

*Ped.*_____

for Ashley, Katie, and Emily

If music be the food of love

William Shakespeare
from *Twelfth Night* (Act 1, Scene 1)

RICHARD ALLAIN
(b. 1965)

Duration: 3.5 mins

Commissioned by Mavis Fletcher on behalf of seven choirs as part of ABCD's Auction 2013
(Cantoris, Carleton Community Chorus, Dorking Camerata, Heyhouses Community Choir,
Lancaster Singers, Southport Bach Choir, and The Maia Singers)

It was a lover and his lass

William Shakespeare
from *As You Like It* (Act 5, Scene 3)

WILL TODD
(b. 1970)

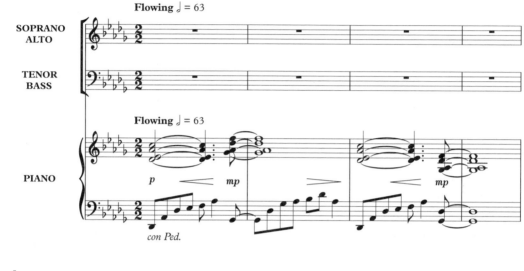

Duration: 3.5 mins

That o'er the green cornfield did pass In

spring-time, spring-time, the on-ly pret-ty ring-time,

When birds do sing, hey sing, ding-a-ding ding,

ding-a-ding ding, Sweet lov-ers love the

* *prime* = the springtime of life/spring/the height of perfection

Shall I compare thee to a summer's day?

William Shakespeare
Sonnet 18

OWAIN PARK
(b. 1993)

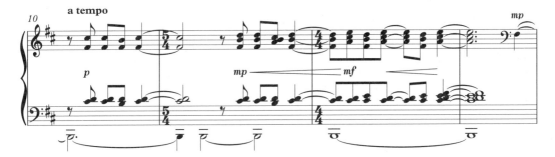

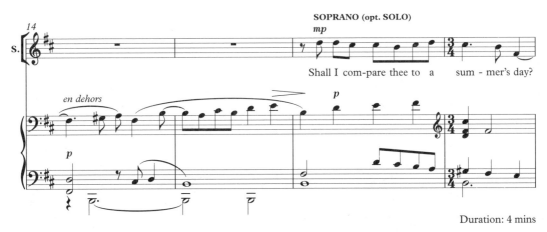

SOPRANO (opt. SOLO)

Shall I com-pare thee to a sum - mer's day?

Duration: 4 mins

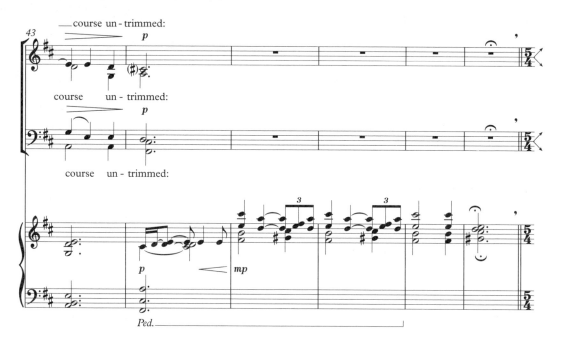

* seamless change to *ah*

this gives life to thee.

this gives life to thee.

meno p

rall.

rall.

mp

p

Ped.

Sigh no more, ladies

William Shakespeare
from *Much Ado About Nothing* (Act 2, Scene 3)

CECILIA McDOWALL
(b. 1951)

Duration: 3 mins

Commissioned by Professor Dame Jessica Rawson
for the Choir of Merton College, Oxford, as part of the Merton Choirbook

The Bird of Dawning

William Shakespeare
from *Hamlet* (Act 1, Scene 1)

BOB CHILCOTT
(b. 1955)

* *'gainst* = towards the time when

Duration: 2.5 mins

* *takes* = bewitches

Touch her soft lips and part

William Shakespeare
from *Henry V* (Act 2, Scene 3)*

WILLIAM WALTON (1902–83)
arr. BOB CHILCOTT (b. 1955)

Duration: 1.5 mins

* The words 'Touch her soft lips and part' were adapted from Shakespeare's 'Touch her soft mouth, and march' for the 1944 film of *Henry V*, for which Walton composed the music.

When that I was and a little tiny boy

William Shakespeare
from *Twelfth Night* (Act 5, Scene 1)

ALAN BULLARD
(b. 1947)

Duration: 2.5 mins

* *and a* = just a

* *swaggering* = blustering, bullying

rain___ it rain - - eth_ ev - 'ry day.___

rain, the rain it rain - - eth_ ev - 'ry_ day.___

(opt. SOLO) *p*

4.But when I came un - to my_ beds,

With

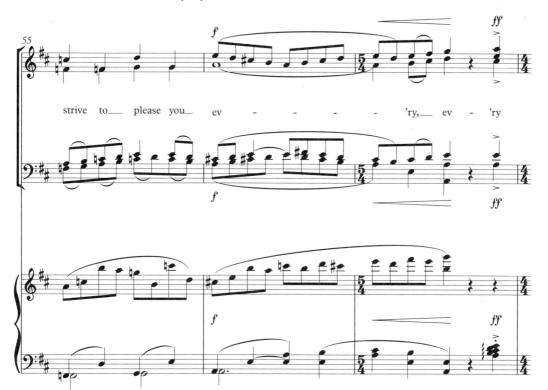

strive to___ please you___ ev - - - - - ’ry,___ ev - ’ry

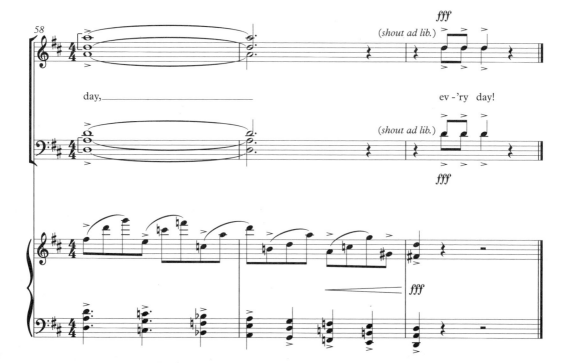

day,_____ ev - ’ry day!